HOORAY FOR
VETERINARIANS!

by Kurt Waldendorf

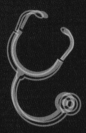

BUMBA BOOKS™

LERNER PUBLICATIONS ◆ MINNEAPOLIS

Note to Educators:

Throughout this book, you'll find critical thinking questions. These can be used to engage young readers in thinking critically about the topic and in using the text and photos to do so.

Lerner Publications Company
A division of Lerner Publishing Group, Inc.
241 First Avenue North
Minneapolis, MN 55401 USA

For reading levels and more information, look up this title at www.lernerbooks.com.

Library of Congress Cataloging-in-Publication Data

Names: Waldendorf, Kurt, author.
Title: Hooray for veterinarians! / by Kurt Waldendorf.
Description: Minneapolis : Lerner Publications, [2017] | Series: Bumba books—Hooray for community helpers! | Audience: Ages 4–8. | Includes bibliographical references and index.
Identifiers: LCCN 2015043697 (print) | LCCN 2015045326 (ebook) | ISBN 9781512414387 (lb : alk. paper) | ISBN 9781512414677 (pb : alk. paper) | ISBN 9781512414684 (eb pdf)
Subjects: LCSH: Veterinarians—Juvenile literature.
Classification: LCC SF756 .W35 2017 (print) | LCC SF756 (ebook) | DDC 636.089092—dc23

LC record available at http://lccn.loc.gov/2015043697

Manufactured in the United States of America
1 – VP – 7/15/16

Expand learning beyond the printed book. Download free, complementary educational resources for this book from our website, www.lernerresource.com.

Table of Contents

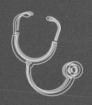

Animal Doctors

Veterinarians are animal doctors.

They are also called vets.

Vets help animals stay healthy.

Vets care for animals. These doctors check animals with tools. Vets know how animal bodies work.

Why might a veterinarian check an animal's ears?

Animals cannot say what hurts.

Vets test animals.

They find out what is wrong

with animals.

Some vets treat big animals.

This horse hurt its leg.

The vet will fix it.

What are some other big animals vets might help?

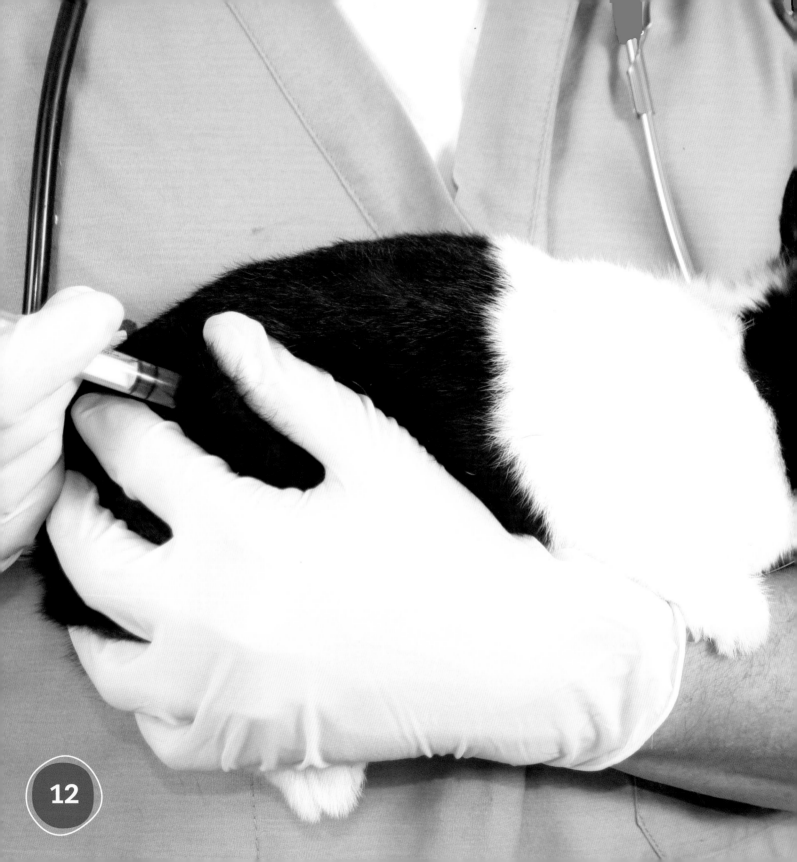

Some vets work with

small animals.

People bring their pets

to the vet.

This vet gives a rabbit

a shot.

Vets help wild animals too.

This bird hurt its wing.

The vet fixed it.

Soon the bird will fly again.

Animals sometimes get scared.

Vets talk to animals.

They pet the animals.

They keep animals calm.

Why do you think visiting the vet scares animals?

Vets work hard.

They go to school for up

to eight years.

They learn how to

be vets.

Vets help many animals.

They keep animals healthy.

Veterinarian Tools

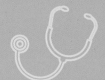

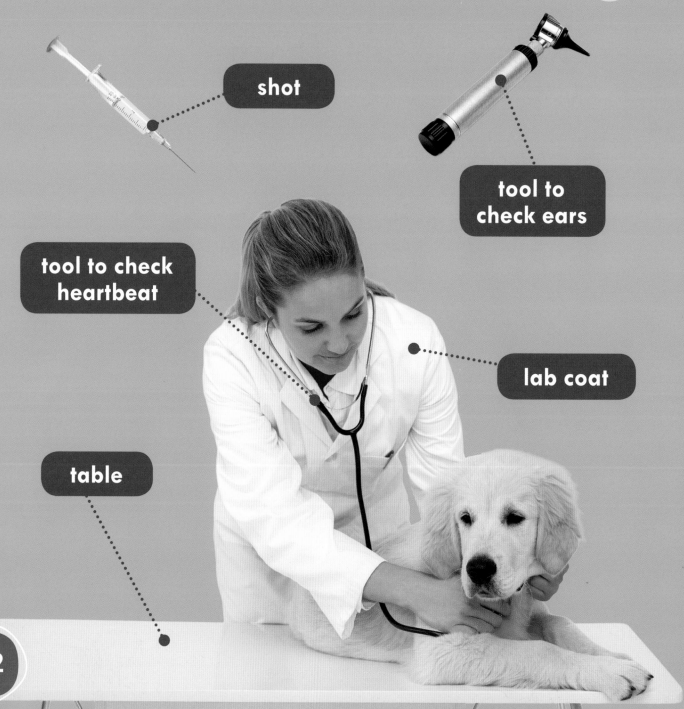

shot

tool to
check ears

tool to check
heartbeat

lab coat

table

Picture Glossary

shot

medicine pushed through a needle

test

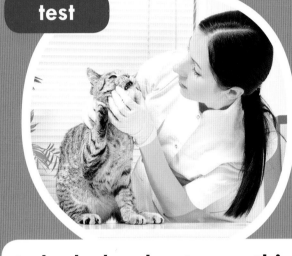

to look closely at something to see what is wrong

veterinarians

doctors who are trained to treat sick or hurt animals

wild animals

animals that live in the wild and are not pets

23

Index

Read More

Bellisario, Gina. *Let's Meet a Veterinarian.* Minneapolis: Millbrook Press, 2013.

Miller, Connie Colwell. *I'll Be a Veterinarian.* Mankato, MN: Amicus, 2016.

Somervil, Barbara A. *Veterinarian.* Ann Arbor, MI: Cherry Lake Publishing, 2016.

Photo Credits